CHARLESTON   L
....

ed on or before the last date

a to Z

Transport

Beverley Mathias
and
Ruth Thomson

Illustrations: Stephen Iliffe

Watts Books
London/New York/Sydney

Watts Books
96 Leonard Street
London EC2A 4RH

Franklin Watts Australia
14 Mars Road
Lane Cove
N.S.W. 2066

© 1988 Franklin Watts
This edition 1995

ISBN: 086313 782 2

Editor: Ruth Thomson
Design: Edward Kinsey

Illustrations © Stephen Iliffe

The authors, illustrator and
Publisher would like to thank the
staff of the Frank Barnes School for
their great help in the preparation
of the Signed English illustrations.

Photographs: Chris Fairclough: A, B,
C, H, I, J, M, Q, S, T, U, X; Zefa: E, F,
G, K, L, N, O, P, R, V, Y, Z; Edward
Kinsey: W; Andy Willsher: D

Typesetting: Lineage, Watford
Printed in Belgium
by Proost International Book Production

About this book

* This book has been designed for use by all people learning to read. It is both an information book and a reading book.

* The alphabet is used to provide a natural framework for the exploration of the book's topic and for language development.

* The simple sentences place the key words in context and extend appreciation of the subject.

* The superb photographs have been carefully selected to stimulate interest and discussion.

* The activities that conclude the book are designed to reinforce understanding and to encourage further involvement in the topic.

* A special feature of the book is the provision of Signed English and the Finger Spelling Alphabet for non-hearing readers. This feature is also intended to provide a fascinating introduction to sign language for all readers, teachers and parents.

Beverley Mathias
Ruth Thomson

Aa

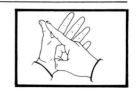

This is the fastest airliner.

This   is   the   fastest   airliner.

Bb

This **bus** takes children to school.

This   bus   takes   children   to   school.

Cc

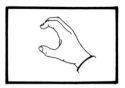

Camels can carry people.

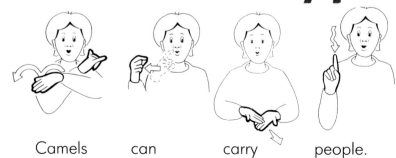

Camels   can   carry   people.

Dd

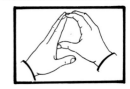

Dragsters are fast racing cars.

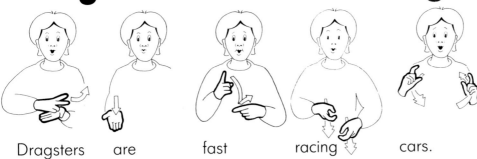

Dragsters   are   fast   racing   cars.

Ee

Escalators are moving staircases.

Escalators   are   moving   staircases.

Ff

People cross this river by ferry.

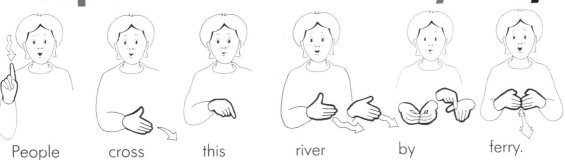

People   cross   this   river   by   ferry.

Gg

Gliders do not have engines.

Gliders   do   not   have   engines.

Hh

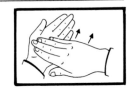

Helicopters can hover.

Helicopters   can   hover.

Ii

Indian canoes are made from logs.

| Indian | canoes | are | made | from | logs. |

Jj

These **jets** are giving a display.

These   jets   are   giving   a   display.

Kk

Kayaks are steered with paddles.

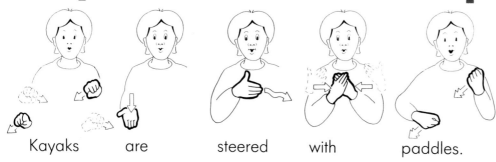

Kayaks   are   steered   with   paddles.

Ll

Liners carry people on holiday.

Liners   carry   people   on   holiday.

Mm

Motorbike stunts are dangerous.

Motorbike   stunts   are   dangerous.

Nn

Racing cars are very noisy.

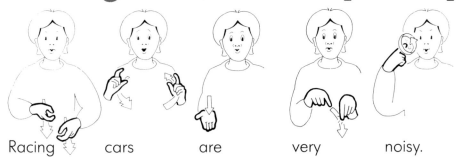

Racing   cars   are   very   noisy.

Oo

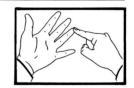

Oil tankers can be gigantic.

Oil   tankers   can   be   gigantic.

Pp

The **parachute floats to earth.**

   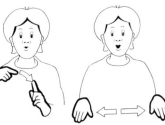

The   parachute   floats   to   earth.

Qq

Cars **queue** to board the ferry.

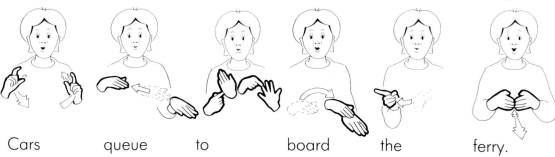

| Cars | queue | to | board | the | ferry. |

Rr

This **roadtrain** is in Australia.

This   roadtrain   is   in   Australia.

Ss

The **ski-lift** goes up the **mountain.**

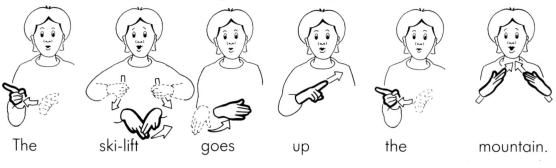

The   ski-lift   goes   up   the   mountain.

Tt

All trains run on tracks.

All   trains   run   on   tracks.

Uu

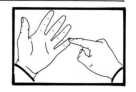

Cities need **underground trains.**

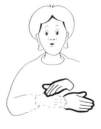

Cities   need   underground trains.

Vv

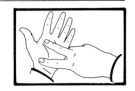

This **vehicle** carries new cars.

This   vehicle   carries   new   cars.

Ww

Windsurfing is fun!

Windsurfing   is   fun!

Xx

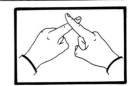

This **ox** is carrying water jars.

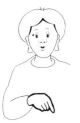     

This   ox   is   carrying   water   jars.

Yy

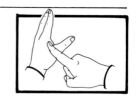

These yachts are having a race.

These   yachts   are   having   a   race.

Zz

The bikes **zoom** round the track.

The   bikes   zoom   round   the   track.

A transport quiz

How many of these questions can you answer?
Look through the book to help you.
The answers are on the last page.

1 Name two kinds of transport which have only two wheels.

2 Which of these is the odd one out? Why?

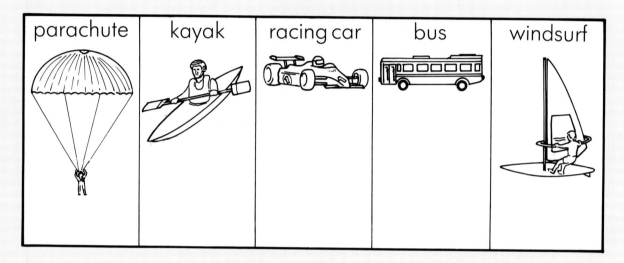

| parachute | kayak | racing car | bus | windsurf |

3 What kind of transport
    a) takes cars from factories to garages?
    b) carries oil from one country to another?
    c) takes skiers up high mountains?

4 Which animal is used to transport people in the desert?

5 Name four kinds of transport which can carry more
    than a hundred people at a time.

6 Which can go faster:
    a) an aeroplane or a glider?
    b) a bicycle or a motorbike?
    c) a ferry or a liner?

7 Which kind of transport:
    a) only goes downwards?
    b) only runs on tracks?

How is it powered?

Do you know what powers different kinds of transport?
Make a chart like the one below. Look through the book and
draw each form of transport in one of the columns of your chart.
Which kind of power is used the most?

muscle power	wind power	oil	electricity

Around the world in eighty ways

(a game for two or more players)

Imagine you and your friends are going on a journey around
the world. You have to travel alternately by land, sea and air.
The first player has to think of a kind of land transport, the next
player has to think of a kind of water transport, and so on. You
can't use any kind of transport that someone has already used.

For example, the first player might say, 'I went around the
world by train.' The second player might say, 'I went round the
world by boat.' The third player might say, 'I went round the
world by glider.'

If you repeat a form of transport someone else has already
used, or if you can't think of a new one, you lose a life. A player
who loses three lives is out of the game.

The Finger Spelling Alphabet

Answers to quiz

1 Bike, motorbike. **2** Bus. All the others can carry only one person at a time.
3 a) Vehicle transporter; b) Oil tanker; c) Ski-lift. **4** Camel. **5** Any four of these: train, airliner, ferry, liner, underground train, ski-lift, escalator. **6** a) Aeroplane; b) Motorbike; c) Liner. **7** a) Parachute; b) Train.